S0-ANQ-639

CHAMPS!
INSPIRATIONAL ANIMALS

Courageous Cats

CHERRY LAKE PRESS
Ann Arbor, Michigan

by Joyce Markovics

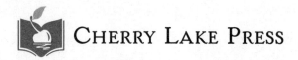

Published in the United States of America by Cherry Lake Publishing
Ann Arbor, Michigan
www.cherrylakepublishing.com

Reading Adviser: Beth Walker Gambro, MS, Ed., Reading Consultant, Yorkville, IL
Content Adviser: William Tavolacci, LVT, CCRP Team Leader, Integrative and Rehabilitative Medicine
Department, Schwarzman Animal Medical Center

Book Designer: Ed Morgan
Book Developer: Bowerbird Books

Photo Credits: © Tosha Bu/Shutterstock, cover and title page; © Casey Elise Christopher/Shutterstock, 5; © Alison Smith, 6 and 7; © Oleksandr Lytvynenko/Shutterstock, 9; © Shine Nucha/Shutterstock, 11; © Sam Tochtrop, 13, 15 top and bottom; © Walkin' Pets, 17; © Siyanight/Shutterstock, 19; freepik.com, 19 bottom; © Rashid Valitov/Shutterstock, 21.

Copyright © 2025 by Cherry Lake Publishing Group

All rights reserved. No part of this book may be reproduced or utilized in any form or by any means without written permission from the publisher.

Cherry Lake Press is an imprint of Cherry Lake Publishing Group.

Library of Congress Cataloging-in-Publication Data has been filed and is available at catalog.loc.gov.

Printed in the United States of America

Note from publisher: Websites change regularly, and their future contents are outside of our control. Supervise children when conducting any recommended online searches for extended learning opportunities.

Contents

Blind BEST FRIEND

Seeing is not always believing. Mowgli the orange tabby cat is proof of that. When he was a kitten, he was found alone on the street. Mowgli was also bumping into things. A vet took him in and called Alison Smith. Alison rescues horses and other animals in need. The vet told Alison that Mowgli's **infected** eyes would need to be removed. When asked if she would give the blind kitten a home after his **surgery**, Alison said yes. "I just had to step in," she said.

After vets removed his eyes, Mowgli quickly healed.

Sometimes, the only way to cure an infection is to remove the infected body part. Doctors perform surgery to do this.

When Alison brought Mowgli home, he was afraid. The blind kitten hardly moved. Eventually, he became more confident. Soon, he found his way around the house. Then, Scarlet joined the family. The small dog also had a **disability**. She had been hit by a car and had trouble walking.

Mowgli and Scarlet often cuddle together in their car seat.

The cat and dog friends go most places together!

Mowgli welcomed Scarlet with open paws. The two animals were drawn to each other. After that, they were **inseparable**! "They have a unique bond that I have never seen before," said Alison. "They eat, sleep, and play together every day." For Mowgli and Scarlet, their friendship is more important than their disabilities.

Extra SPECIAL CATS

Blindness is one of many disabilities affecting cats. Having a disability can make it hard to see, walk, hear, or learn. Some animals are born with disabilities. Others might have an illness or injury that causes them to become disabled.

In the past, disabled cats often had hard lives. Things are different today. There are many ways to assist these special cats. With a little help from humans, cats with disabilities can live long, healthy lives. And they can make loving pets!

There are many different kinds of cats.
They range in size, color, and fur length.

A physical disability affects the body. A
mental disability **impacts** the brain or mind.

Cool
KITTIES

Scooter is a loving and unique pet. This kitty was born with a spine problem. As a result, her hind legs are **paralyzed**. Sam Tochtrop, a doctor, rescued Scooter. He knew caring for her would be a lot of work. But he wanted to give Scooter a good life. "I was willing to put in the work," Sam said.

To get around, Scooter used her front legs to drag herself. "The very first thing I did was make her a ramp so she could get on my bed," said Sam. "She took extremely fast to it." That was one of many things Sam did to help Scooter. But Scooter also helped herself.

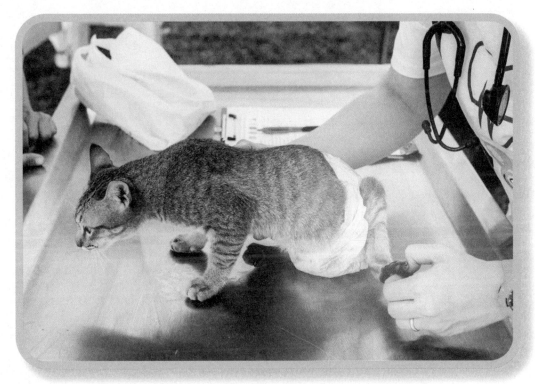

This paralyzed cat is being examined by a veterinarian.

Scooter got her name because she scoots, or slides, across the floor.

One day, Scooter surprised Sam. She pulled herself up the stairs all on her own! "This was a **monumental** moment," said Sam. "This made me realize that Scooter is capable of so much." Sam then made Scooter a cat tower with a ramp. He called it the "Scootbutt Snooze Hut." It gave the kitty a place to rest and look out the window. Right away, Scooter climbed inside. "She has her own special needs," said Sam. "But she doesn't wait for my permission to climb, jump, or explore something new!"

Sam took a video of Scooter climbing the stairs. It has been viewed by tens of thousands of people!

Scooter the incredible cat

13

Being a doctor and caring for Scooter isn't easy. However, Sam loves every minute. He couldn't be happier and prouder to have a cat like Scooter. And he believes she has taught him to be a better doctor. "I used to hate cats, and I didn't understand them," Sam said. "Scooter helped me to tap into a bit of **compassion** that I didn't have before." Sam has also learned how to **adapt** to Scooter's—and his patients'—needs. Every living thing has special needs!

Scooter taught Sam that compassion
is a big part of being a good doctor.

In his free time, Sam makes dolls inspired by his cat.
The dolls have legs that are shaped just like Scooter's!

Holly is another courageous cat. When she was a couple of months old, rescuers found her struggling to walk. They took her to a vet. There, she was **diagnosed** with a brain issue. It's called Wobbly Cat Syndrome. "These cats can live long and healthy lives," said one vet. "They just look a bit funny when they walk around."

When Barb Hun saw Holly's picture, she knew she wanted to **adopt** the black cat. Barb also wanted to help Holly walk. So, she got in touch with Walkin' Pets. The company builds **mobility aids** for animals. Holly soon got her very own wheelchair—and her life changed! She now zooms around the house. "She inspires people with her **determination**," said Barb.

Holly is dressed up for Halloween in her specially designed set of wheels!

To the Rescue!

There are people—and organizations—across the country that help cats in need. Milo's **Sanctuary** is **devoted** to caring for disabled cats. Many of Milo's special needs kitties find homes. Some, however, have severe disabilities or illnesses. So Milo's cares for them! The rescue gives these extra special cats a safe, loving home for the rest of their lives.

All cats need care and love, especially disabled ones.

There are dozens of cats in the lifetime care program. Cabitha Toffeetoes is one. She was born with misshapen front legs. Earl is another kitty. He was hit by a car and has a broken jaw. Today, the cats are thriving. And they're enjoying the care they deserve.

There are hundreds of cat rescues in the United States.

Little Wanderers is another cat rescue. It was founded in 2017. The group's mission is to help the neediest cats in New York City. One day, a cat with serious health issues was found on the street. Despite her small size, she had a big belly. **Volunteers** from Little Wanderers rescued her and named her Free. A couple of weeks later, Free gave birth to a litter of kittens. Free is a great mom. Thanks to Little Wanderers, she and her babies will find forever homes!

A mother cat feeds her kittens.

Animal Nation is another rescue organization in New York. They help 350 cats find loving homes each year!

Adopting a DISABLED Animal

Animals with disabilities aren't often adopted. Here are some reasons to welcome a disabled animal into your home!

- **Save Lives**
  Because of their special needs, disabled animals are more likely to be **euthanized** in shelters. Pet adoption can save lives.

- **Companionship**
  Disabled animals provide companionship. They can form very close bonds with their human caregivers.

- **Special Abilities**
  Animals with disabilities can have hidden strengths. For example, a blind animal may have enhanced senses of hearing and smell.

- **Inspire Others**
  Adopting a disabled animal might inspire someone else to do the same!

Glossary

adapt (uh-DAPT) to change in order to face new settings and challenges

adopt (uh-DOPT) to take into one's family

compassion (kuhm-PASH-uhn) concern or sympathy for another living thing

determination (di-ter-min-AY-shun) the desire and drive to complete something

devoted (dih-VOH-tid) very loving or loyal

diagnosed (dye-uhg-NOHSSD) determined what disease or illness an animal has and what the cause is

disability (diss-uh-BIL-uh-tee) a condition that makes it hard to do certain things, such as walking, seeing, or hearing

euthanized (YOO-thuh-nyezd) painlessly ended the life of a suffering animal

impacts (IM-pakts) strongly affects something

infected (in-FEK-tid) filled with harmful germs

inseparable (in-SEP-er-uh-buhl) two things that are very closely connected

mobility aids (mo-BIH-luh-tee AYDZ) tools that help an animal or person move

monumental (mon-yuh-MEN-tuhl) of great size or importance

paralyzed (PA-ruh-lized) unable to move parts of one's body

sanctuary (SANGK-choo-er-ee) a place where animals are cared for and protected

surgery (SUR-jur-ee) an operation that treats injuries or diseases by fixing or removing body parts

volunteers (vol-uhn-TEERZ) people who help others for no pay

Find Out More

BOOKS

125 Animals That Changed the World. Washington, DC: National Geographic Kids, 2019.

Newman, Aline Alexander, and Gary Weitzman, D.V.M. *How to Speak Cat*. Washington, DC: National Geographic, 2015.

Wheeler-Toppen, Jodi. *Cat Science Unleashed.* Washington, DC: National Geographic, 2019.

WEBSITES
Explore these online sources with an adult:

Britannica Kids: Cat

The Dodo—Special Needs Cat

National Geographic Kids: Cats Memory Game

Index

About the Author

Joyce Markovics is passionate about books and animals. She would like to thank Bill Tavolacci, Alison Smith, Sam Tochtrop, and Walkin' Pets for helping disabled animals live fuller, happier lives.